STARS OF SPORTS

MEGAN
RAPINOE

WORLD CUP CHAMPION

by Matt Chandler

CAPSTONE PRESS
a capstone imprint

Capstone Captivate is published by Capstone Press, an imprint of Capstone.
1710 Roe Crest Drive
North Mankato, Minnesota 56003
www.capstonepub.com

Library of Congress Cataloging-in-Publication Data is available on the Library of Congress website.
ISBN: 978-1-4966-8386-1 (hardcover)
ISBN: 978-1-4966-8437-0 (eBook PDF)

Summary: As a child, Megan Rapinoe watched her brother play soccer. It wasn't long before she was kicking the ball around. Since then, she has gained much success, and the left-winger is now known as a leader on and off the field. Discover Rapinoe's journey to becoming a world star in this thrilling biography in the Stars of Sports series.

Image Credits
Getty Images: FIFA/Stuart Franklin, 20, ISI Photos/Brad Smith, 28; Newscom: ABACA/ PA Photos/EMPICS Sport, 22, 23, Icon SMI/Andy Mead, 10, Icon SMI/Richard Clement, 11, Icon SMI/Scott Bales, 13, Icon SMI/YCJ/Andy Mead, 16, Icon Sportswire/ David J. Griffin, 25, Icon Sportswire/Diego Diaz, 17, picture-alliance/dpa/Jens Wolf, 15, Reuters/Chaiwat Subprasom, 9, UPI/David Silpa, 5; Shutterstock: Cody Markhart, 7, feelphoto, 18, Pierre Teyssot, 19, Romain Biard, cover, tarabird, 26, winui, 1

Editorial Credits
Editor: Gena Chester; Designer: Elyse White; Media Researcher: Eric Gohl; Production Specialist: Laura Manthe

All internet sites appearing in back matter were available and accurate when this book was sent to press.

Direct Quotations
Page 6, "I was always so . . ." Kevin Koczwara, "An Interview with Megan Rapinoe," October 1, 2015, https://believermag.com/an-interview-with-megan-rapinoe/Accessed on March 10, 2020.

Page 21, "The semifinal was just . . ." NPR, "Megan Rapinoe on Winning Gold, Soccer's Future," August 15, 2012, https://www.npr.org/2012/08/15/158887977/soccer-star-rapinoe-on-winning-gold
Accessed on March 10, 2020.

Page 25, "I felt like it . . ." ESPN Originals, "Megan Rapinoe Discusses Why She Will Kneel in a USWNT Jersey," https://www.youtube.com/watch?v=-dO6GMqhKFk
Accessed on March 10, 2020.

Page 27, "We have to be . . ." Alexandra Licata, "'We Have to Love More. Hate Less': Megan Rapinoe delivered a powerful speech at the USWNT parade," https://www.businessinsider.com/megan-rapinoe-speech-uswnt-celebration-fifa-world-cup-2019-7
Accessed on March 10, 2020.

Printed in the United States of America.
PA117

TABLE OF CONTENTS

CHAMPIONS!... 4

CHAPTER ONE
BEFORE FAME... 6

CHAPTER TWO
RISING STAR... 10

CHAPTER THREE
PROFESSIONAL PLAY............................... 14

CHAPTER FOUR
OLYMPIC HERO!.................................... 21

CHAPTER FIVE
MORE THAN AN ATHLETE 24

TIMELINE 29
GLOSSARY. 30
READ MORE 31
INTERNET SITES 31
INDEX. 32

Glossary terms are **BOLD** on first use.

In 2019, the United States Women's National Team was favored to win the World Cup. The team faced the Netherlands in the finals. The two teams were locked in a scoreless battle for 60 minutes. The U.S. drew a penalty kick, and Megan Rapinoe had a chance to give her team the lead.

As goalkeeper Sari van Veenendaal took a slight step to her right, Rapinoe pounced. She drilled a kick to the goalie's left. Goal! The U.S. took a 1–0 lead. The Netherlands never caught up. Rapinoe and her teammates won the game 2–0. Rapinoe scored the game-winning kick to give the U.S. its fourth FIFA World Cup!

FACT

Rapinoe was the leading scorer, with six goals, in the 2019 World Cup. She won the Golden Boot award as the top scorer.

CHAPTER ONE

BEFORE FAME

Megan Rapinoe grew up in California. She is one of six children, including her twin sister, Rachael. Megan was only three when she began to show interest in soccer. Her mom was the coach of her brother Brian's team. Megan and Rachael would go to his games.

The next year, the twins played at an old church across from their house. Brian taught them everything he knew about the game.

"I was always so excited to go and play soccer," Rapinoe said in a 2015 interview. "I loved it."

That love was what drove Megan to the next level. She had her sights set on playing in high school, and hopefully earning a **scholarship** to play in college.

⟨⟨⟨ Megan's hometown, Redding, California

All in the Family

Megan wanted to be just like her big brother. She played left wing because Brian did. She wore number seven because that was his number. But when Megan was 10 years old, things changed. Brian was arrested and went to prison. Megan stayed in touch through letters. Today, they each credit the other one for inspiring them to be the best they can be.

NATIONAL NOISE

By the time Megan reached high school, she had become a star on the soccer **pitch**. But there weren't any top-level teams to play on in her town. So she chose to play for Elk Grove Pride. The club team was located about three hours from Megan's home. Megan's family supported her passion for the game. Her parents drove 300 miles each way for every practice and game.

Megan's success on her club team earned her national attention. In 2004, she was named a McDonald's All-American player. She also earned All-American honors in her junior and senior high-school seasons. Rapinoe was ready to take her game to college!

Rapinoe (center) battles for the ball against ⟩⟩⟩ a Brazil player in a U-19 Women's World Championships third-place match.

FIFA Star

Rapinoe took a pass from the corner in the 2004 FIFA U-19 World Championships. She quickly blasted a shot that curled over the arms of the Brazilian goaltender, Thaís, and into the net. The goal gave the U.S. a 2–0 lead in its final match. Rapinoe helped the United States' U-19 team to victory at the 2004 tournament. Her performance paved the way for her spot on the World Cup team two years later.

CHAPTER TWO

RISING STAR

Rapinoe chose to attend the University of Portland. She shared the field with her twin sister, Rachael. In Rapinoe's first season, she scored 43 points.

In her second season, Rapinoe led the country in goals through her first 11 games. Then, disaster struck. She tore the **ACL** in her left knee. Her season was over.

》》》 Rapinoe (3) fights for a header in a University of Portland game against the University of North Carolina.

〉〉〉 Rapinoe throws the ball in during
a college match.

In her third year at Portland, she was ready to pick up where she had left off. But two games into her return, she tore the same ACL. The repeated injury meant the end of her college career.

UNITED STATES WOMEN'S NATIONAL TEAM

In 2006, after she recovered from the second knee injury, Rapinoe joined the United States Women's National Team. A few months later, she delivered her first of many goals on the team.

The U.S. was playing Chinese Taipei in a **friendly**. The U.S. had such a big lead that Rapinoe came onto the pitch as a **rookie**. She trailed teammate Abby Wambach, who fed her a pass across the front of the goal. The Chinese Taipei goaltender was out of position. Rapinoe knocked the ball into the net for her first goal in **international** play. She added a second goal later in the game. The U.S. won 10–0.

It's been more than 10 years since Rapinoe's first goal. She's played in more than 150 matches for the U.S. women's team. In 2019, she scored the 50th international goal of her career!

》》》 Rapinoe takes the ball past a Chinese
Taipei player in a 2006 friendly.

CHAPTER THREE

PROFESSIONAL PLAY

On the U.S. women's team, Rapinoe appeared in her first FIFA World Cup match in 2011. There, she made an incredible assist. The U.S. trailed Brazil 2–1 late in a semifinal match. It looked like the team was going to be eliminated. Then the U.S. pulled out a miracle.

Rapinoe carried the ball up the field. As Abby Wambach moved toward the net, Rapinoe sent a perfect pass. The ball sailed high toward the right corner of the goal. It arrived at the exact moment Wambach did. She delivered an easy header into the net. The goal tied the game! The U.S. later lost to Japan in the finals. But Rapinoe's pass is remembered as one of the biggest moments in World Cup history.

 Rapinoe and Abby Wambach celebrate after Wambach's goal in the 2011 FIFA World Cup semifinal match.

FACT

Wambach's goal holds the record for the latest goal ever scored in a World Cup game. She netted the header in the 122nd minute of play.

NATIONAL STAGE

Most of Rapinoe's fame comes from playing on the international stage. World Cup titles and Olympic medals are exciting. But outside of those moments, Rapinoe perfects her skills playing professional club soccer in the United States.

〉〉〉 Rapinoe was chosen by the Chicago Red Stars at the 2009 WPS Draft.

〉〉〉 Rapinoe (right) playing for the Seattle Reign
in a game against the Portland Thorns in 2015

Rapinoe's pro career began in 2009. The Chicago
Red Stars selected her in the first round of the 2009
Women's Professional Soccer (WPS) **Draft**. She played
two seasons in Chicago. She joined the Seattle Reign
FC in 2013. In her pro career, she's scored 53 goals.
Thirty-seven of those were with Seattle.

Women's soccer is a totally different game at the
club level than the international level. Seattle plays in a
stadium that holds fewer than 7,000 fans. In the World
Cup, Rapinoe plays in front of more than 50,000 fans.

RETURN TO THE CUP

Rapinoe is a fierce competitor. The World Cup loss in 2011 hurt. The U.S. had to wait four years for a rematch. In 2015, the team got its second chance. Rapinoe scored two goals in the tournament. The U.S. once again faced Japan in the final match. This time around, the U.S. took home the championship. It defeated Japan 5–2.

〉〉〉 Rapinoe in a 2019 Women's World Cup game against Thailand

>>> Along with the Golden Ball and the World Cup
championship trophy, she won the Golden Boot.

At 34 years old, Rapinoe should have been a
part-time bench player in the 2019 World Cup.
Instead, she played some of the best soccer of her
career. She scored six goals in the tournament. The
U.S. beat the Netherlands to win back-to-back World
Cup titles. Rapinoe earned the Golden Ball award as
the tournament's Most Valuable Player (MVP).

CHAPTER FOUR

OLYMPIC HERO!

Rapinoe was still recovering from her second ACL tear when players were selected for the 2008 Olympic team. She was determined to make the 2012 team. It was her dream since she was growing up in California.

Her knee was fully recovered for the 2012 Olympics in London. The first-time Olympian performed well. She scored her first Olympic goal in the team's second match against Colombia. The U.S. won 3–0. In the semifinals, Rapinoe added two more goals in a huge 4–3 win over Canada.

"The semifinal was just insane," Rapinoe said. "The energy in the stadium was just rising with every minute, and I thought it was great for women's football."

⟨⟨⟨ Rapinoe heads the ball in the semifinal match against Canada.

STRIKING GOLD

Not every big moment means scoring a goal. In the 2012 gold medal match, Rapinoe made a needed play. The U.S. held a 1–0 lead over Japan. But the Japanese team was aggressive. It had several great attempts on the U.S. goal. The U.S. needed another goal to take the pressure off.

Rapinoe brought the ball up the field. She saw Carli Lloyd on her right, sneaking up the middle. Rapinoe hit her with a perfect pass, and Lloyd did the rest. She weaved through the defense and delivered a shot. The kick hooked toward the left corner of the goal and in!

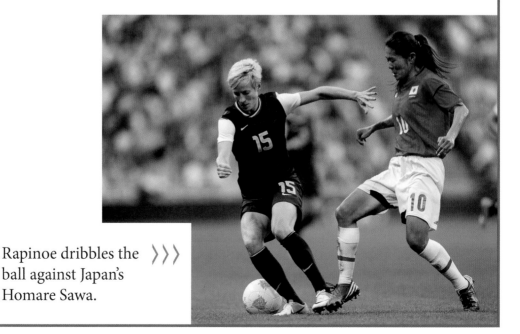

Rapinoe dribbles the ball against Japan's Homare Sawa. 〉〉〉

The U.S. held on for a 2–1 win. Rapinoe was credited with an assist on the game-winning goal. She was now an Olympic gold medalist!

>>> Rapinoe celebrates winning the gold medal at the 2012 Olympic Games.

CHAPTER FIVE
MORE THAN AN ATHLETE

Rapinoe is more than just a soccer player. She is a **social activist**. Rapinoe has spoken out on everything from equality in sports to LGBTQ rights. But it was a moment in September 2016 for which she will always be remembered.

The U.S. was about to play Thailand. U.S. Air Force Master Sergeant Alyson Jones took the field to sing the National Anthem. As her teammates lined up and placed their hands over their hearts, Rapinoe did not. Instead, she dropped to one knee in protest.

The move was seen by many as disrespectful of the military and of the United States. Rapinoe and her supporters saw it differently. After the game, she explained her decision.

>>> Rapinoe kneeled during the National Anthem
before a 2016 U.S. women's team game in 2016.

"I felt like it was the right thing to do," she said. "I
am gay, and I feel like I have a level of **empathy** in just
not having all of my rights protected."

FACT

In 2019, Rapinoe was named co-captain of the
U.S. women's team. She shared the role with
teammates Carli Lloyd and Alex Morgan.

》》》 Rapinoe holds up the Women's World
Cup trophy at a New York parade in 2019.

BEYOND THE PITCH

When Rapinoe decides to hang up her cleats, she will have many opportunities outside of the game she loves. She is known as much for her work off the field as she is for her play on it. Many people think her social activism is courageous.

Rapinoe has used her new fame off the pitch to inspire change. She is a powerful public speaker. At a parade in 2019, Rapinoe gave a passionate speech. She challenged people to think about how they could make a difference in the world.

"We have to be better. We have to love more. Hate less," she told the crowd. "It's our responsibility to make this world a better place."

FACT

Rapinoe is one of the leaders in a **lawsuit** filed against the United States Soccer Federation. The lawsuit seeks the same pay and working conditions as the men's national team.

A LASTING LEGACY

Two World Cup titles, an Olympic gold medal, fame and fortune—soccer star Megan Rapinoe has accomplished much in her career. She is one of the greatest players in the game today. History will remember Rapinoe as a famous soccer player. Her fans will remember her as a person who fought for fairness and equality in the world. Best of all, Rapinoe isn't finished. She plans to play for the World Cup team in 2023. At an age where most players retire, Rapinoe keeps getting better!

TIMELINE

1985 Megan Anna Rapinoe is born in Redding, California, on July 5.

2002 Makes her debut playing for the Elk Grove Pride of the Women's Premier Soccer League

2004 Enrolls at the University of Portland on a full soccer scholarship to play for the Portland Pilots

2006 Named to the United States Women's National Team

2009 Drafted in the first round (second overall) by the Chicago Red Stars of the Women's Professional Soccer League

2011 Scores her first World Cup goal in a game against Colombia

2012 Wins a gold medal as a member of the United States Women's National Team at the London Olympics

2015 Leads the U.S. team as it wins the FIFA Women's World Cup

2019 Named the Sports Illustrated Sportsperson of the Year

2019 Wins her second FIFA World Cup, the Golden Ball award as MVP, and the Golden Boot award as top scorer

GLOSSARY

ACL (AY-SEE-EL)—stands for "anterior cruciate ligament;" a key connective tissue that helps to keep the knee joint steady

DRAFT (DRAFT)—the process of choosing a person to join a sports team

EMPATHY (EM-puh-thee)—imagining how others feel

FRIENDLY (FREND-lee)—a game that is played outside of a tournament or league

INTERNATIONAL (in-tur-NASH-uh-nuhl)—between or among the nations of the world

LAWSUIT (LAW-soot)—a legal action or case brought against a person or group in a court of law

PITCH (PICH)—a soccer field

ROOKIE (RUK-ee)—a first-year player

SCHOLARSHIP (SKOL-ur-ship)—money given to a student to pay for school

SOCIAL ACTIVIST (SOH-shuhl ak-TUH-vuhst)—a person who takes organized action to improve a community

READ MORE

Carothers, Thomas. *Pro Soccer Upsets.* Minneapolis: Lerner Publishing, 2020.

Chandler, Matt. *Alex Morgan: Soccer Champion.* North Mankato, MN: Capstone Press, 2020.

Williams, Heather. *Soccer: A Guide for Players and Fans.* North Mankato, MN: Capstone Press, 2020.

INTERNET SITES

Major League Soccer
www.mlssoccer.com

National Women's Soccer League
www.nwslsoccer.com

United States Women's National Team
www.ussoccer.com/teams/uswnt

INDEX

awards, 4, 8, 19

Brazil, 9, 14

California, 6, 21
Canada, 21
Chicago Red Stars, 17
Chinese Taipei, 12
Colombia, 21

drafts, 17

family, 6, 7, 8
fans, 17, 28
FIFA U-19 World
   Championships, 9
friendlies, 12

injuries, 10, 11, 21

Japan, 14, 18, 22

lawsuits, 27
Lloyd, Carli, 22, 25

Morgan, Alex, 25
Most Valuable Player (MVP),
   19

Netherlands, the, 4, 19

Olympics, 16, 21, 22, 23, 28

protesting, 24
public speaking, 27

records, 15

scholarships, 6
schooling, 6, 8, 10, 11
Seattle Reign FC, 17
social activism, 24, 27

Thailand, 24
Thaís, 9

United States Women's
   National Team, 4, 12, 14, 18,
   19, 24, 25

Veenendaal, Sari van, 4

Wambach, Abby, 12, 14
World Cups, 4, 9, 14, 15, 16,
   17, 18, 19, 28